The

Little Guide

for

Hope & Help

Written by

ADRIAN EVERITT

Copyright © 2020 by Adrian Everitt

All rights reserved. No part of this publication may be reproduced, distributed, or transmitted in any form or by any means, including photocopying, recording, or other electronic or mechanical methods, without the prior written permission of the publisher, except in the case of brief quotations embodied in critical reviews and certain other noncommercial uses permitted by copyright law.

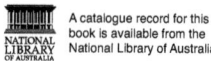

A catalogue record for this book is available from the National Library of Australia

Everitt, Adrian *(author)*

The Little Guide of Hope & Help

978-1-922452-85-6

SELF-HELP / Spirituality

Typeset Hero 8/12

Cover and book design by Green Hill Publishing

The Little Guide for Hope & Help

Contents

Introduction	1
Chapter One: Adversity	5
Chapter Two: Healing	7
Chapter Three: Always Be Kind	13
Chapter Four: Don't Worry, Be Happy!	21
Chapter Five: Affirmations	29
Chapter Six: Intuition	35
Chapter Seven: Just Be Yourself	39
Chapter Eight: Bad Readings, Phonies and Dream Catchers	45
Chapter Nine: The Unemployment Blues	55
Chapter Ten: How to Deal with a Toxic Person	61
Chapter Eleven: A Little Less ...	73
Chapter Twelve: Start A New Life!	77
Chapter Thirteen: Establish A Routine	81
Chapter Fourteen: Prayers	87
Conclusion	93

Introduction

From a young age I have encountered the paranormal. I have had spiritual experiences, coincidences and synchronicities within the spiritual realm. If you are reading this for the first time, you may be interested to know that this is actually my second book. My first book was published in June 2019.

Since I wrote my last book, my life hasn't been very good. In fact, it's been heartbreaking. I went from having everything to losing everything in the space of five months, from June to October 2019. I had been dealing with a toxic person. As of January 2020, however, things slowly started to improve for me. I changed my mentality, becoming more determined and resilient, and decided not to give up. With the knowledge I already had and lessons learnt from this recent experience, I have been bouncing back!

I am stubborn, determined, strong-willed. These personal traits of mine helped me to plough through this horrible time. And I had patience because I knew that after all I had been through, surely there would be some positives waiting for me once the hard time cleared away.

I am a clairsentient, intuitive, empathic fortune teller. I learnt all of this about myself when I was younger, and that I was meant to be a spiritually gifted person in this lifetime. I am known for being a spiritual, cheerful, energetic person, with a sense of humour as well. I've recently been reminded that not everybody is going to like me and not everybody is going like my style of work either. In fact, some probably think I am in the same league as the devil!

My Cosmic Answers Facebook page is going well and is popular still. As for my readings and my market stall, that's not such good news. I found it hard to get my Cosmic Answers brand up and running while living out in a rural area. I also became busy working in paid employment; and that took away the time to do readings, which is what I enjoy doing and makes me happy. It's May 2020 as I write this introduction, and I am ready to make my comeback.

This main purpose of this book will be slightly different to the purpose of my first book. This is more of a self-help and educational guide. In Chapter Ten I'll tell you about my experience in dealing with a narcissist, talk about ways to tackle a toxic person, and outline the steps I took for survival. I'll teach you some things to assist you with your journey through your life, and I will teach you what I know within the spiritual realm and from my life experiences.

I am writing this book to give you - or perhaps somebody you know - hope, motivation and inspiration. If those three things can be brought to your life or theirs, you can get through whatever you're dealing with. Nothing would make me happier than to one day meet somebody who says that my book has benefited them in some way. All I want to do is care, be caring and kind. Throughout my life I've just wanted to help people. Those close to me know this about me.

Please pass on my book to somebody if you have finished it and think it may help them. I hope you enjoy reading my second book.

Chapter One
Adversity

Have the confidence to stand in the face of adversity!

Know that the Divine has got your back and that beyond your challenges there is a bigger breakthrough in store for you.

There could be forces that are stopping you from receiving your best life, but decide to stand up or speak up, knowing your faith is bigger than your fear. Fear is an illusion that's trying to hold you down, but will soon disappear.

You become stronger and wiser when you step out in faith. The lessons brought about by all the people and situations we come into contact with mean that they are our teachers and exams. Take the opportunity to get an A-plus!

Chapter Two
Healing

Amongst my spiritual gifts and abilities, another quality I have is healing. I have been told by other spiritual people within the realm that I am a healer and capable of healing people.

Healing in a spiritual way is a connection of spirit and energy. The spiritual person may be a reiki practitioner, a psychic or a medium. That person will attract a universal life force energy with their psychic senses, then draw that into their client to heal them. The healer will connect with their spirit guides, angels and other helpers in order to heal and assist the client. The healer may also be guided by their spiritual guides about what healing work needs to be done for the client.

Before healing a client, the healer needs to make sure that they have a clean energy field, their chakras are balanced and aligned, and they have a pure channel. Why?

If your healer has unbalanced energy or chakras, the negative energy or entities around them will affect your healing and it will not be of a good quality for you.

What happens when this occurs?

It will need to be removed and fixed. But it should not happen in the first place, as the healer should be reliable and trustworthy.

*Why would you or others need
or want a healing?*

Basically, a healing is required when the person has experienced significant mental, emotional or physical pain or trauma. People may need or require a healing from bad relationships, traumatic events or natural disasters (or many other things - the list can go on and on), because these things can cause stress and anxiety. A healing is one part of the process for becoming a happier, healthier person again.

To be honest, I do more intuitive card readings for my clients than I do healings. Yes, I would like to do healing in the future, and eventually offer it as another service through my Cosmic Answers business.

Here are a few simple, basic things you can do to heal yourself and feel better again:

SLEEP: When you're sick or run down, make sure you are getting plenty of proper, undisturbed sleep.

REST: Lounge about all day at home and wear your pyjamas all day. Basically, do nothing. Just let your mind, body and soul chill out and recharge and refuel.

MUSIC: Listen to your favourite musicians, bands and singers, to help you heal and raise your vibrations again.

EAT HEALTHY: If you are really sick or run down, drink juices or have soups. You have to consume something to get better. To regain your strength and energy, it's important to start with fresh fruits and vegetables, even if it's a small quantity to start with.

MEDITATION: Calm your mind, body and soul by meditating. Take some time to be still and clear the clutter from your mind for a while. Meditate daily if possible - when you are healing it certainly helps. It can be for 15 minutes each time.

STAY HYDRATED: Drink plenty of water. If you are unwell or burnt out, just do the best you can to drink as much as you can, to keep your fluids up. Drinking teas and juices can also help you feel better.

IF YOU ARE UNDER PRESSURE: Don't stress yourself out or get into stressful situations. Take it easy on yourself. Heartbreak hurts, words can hurt, and doing too much can hurt as well.

SAY AFFIRMATIONS: Keep those thoughts positive and you will get through whatever you're going through. Think positive and say positive things. Start with affirmations, which will help you to become more positive in your healing process and recovery.

COMFORT FOOD: I know I said earlier that you should eat healthy when you are healing yourself. But when I was in a bad place, I lost count of the amount of Vegan Ben and Jerry tubs I ate! Everything in moderation is the key, so treat yourself to your favourite snacks or beverages once in a while, whilst still trying to get that healthy lifestyle back.

SWITCH OFF: Switch off the mobile phone. Switch off the radio. Switch off the computer or TV. I don't mean to switch them off completely or entirely whilst you are healing, but it does help to take a break from them. Just take no calls or messages and don't look at social media for a while, and detox.

When it comes to healing, the prayer in Chapter Fourteen can be helpful. It's not a miracle cure but it is another way to assist in your healing. It sends out to your Spirit Guides and helpers the message that you are in need of assistance.

Even if it hurts, be brave enough to heal yourself, whatever you've been through or are going through, or whatever has broken your heart or your soul. I hope this chapter has been helpful for you. It takes time to heal, but you can recover and live your life to the fullest.

Chapter Three
Always Be Kind

As a clairsentient I can feel, sense, and just know if somebody isn't happy or if something is wrong with them. I can sense a person's feelings, thoughts, pain and emotions without their having to speak to me. All I can do for them is to understand, acknowledge how they are feeling, and ask if they would like to talk about it.

There have been times when I've been overwhelmed by the bad energy or vibes coming from one or more people near to where I am. At times I've felt my energy being drained from me and have felt worn out.

What happens when I feel like this?

I take time out for myself and have a break for ten minutes or so. I get some fresh air, clear my head, then come back to what I was doing.

It is important to be positive, to put out positive energy or vibes into your mind, home, work place, and everywhere in general. Sometimes this is easier said than done, but try your best to think positively and to be positive. What you send out into the world around you comes back to you. If you put out negative thoughts, energies and vibes, you will get negative in return. What kind of vibes are you sending out?

When you're being kind, be careful. Don't just dive in and rescue somebody. Not everybody wants to be saved. Save your energy, time and kindness for somebody who genuinely wants it and will appreciate it and your good karma. Being psychic, I see things differently. I can see the good, bad and ugly within people, places and situations, so the empath within me wants to go to their rescue and help, to try and fix things for them and make them a better person. This isn't my responsibility, nor should it be yours.

If you want to show your support and kindness to somebody, here are some communication skills that might help:

- Make appropriate eye contact;

- Face each other when you are talking - don't gaze down at your phone or out a window;

- Be present in the conversation and show that you are listening and do care; this will help you gain better understanding of the person and their situation;

- Be a good listener to what the person is talking to you about, whether it is about a certain person or situation;

- To show that you are listening and acknowledge and understand someone who is speaking to you, repeat back to them what they have said;

- Ask the person how they feel about something;

- Be mindful of your tone when speaking to a person, as some tones of voice may impact them and upset or anger them.

What kind things can you do? Here are some examples:

THINK BEFORE YOU SPEAK: Use encouraging, loving and kind words. Find something nice to say about that person. Can you rephrase what you'd like to say in a more positive way?

SET AN EXAMPLE: Be a good person; be that kind person by saying nice things and kind things, and make kind and positive gestures.

FEEL GOOD: Yes - feel good about your words and actions, making sure they have positive intentions, and have a positive impact. What you put out comes back to you.

HOLD A DOOR OPEN FOR THE OTHER PERSON: This is not something see often these days, but some people still do it; it's a kind gesture that shouldn't go unappreciated.

CHECK ON YOUR NEIGHBOUR: If you see your neighbour outside, give them a wave; maybe say hello, make small talk; check on them to see if they are okay or if they need anything.

COMPLIMENT SOMEBODY: Say something nice to somebody, make them feel good and brighten their day. But be careful with making some compliments - it could land you in trouble!

BRING FOOD TO SHARE AT WORK: This is one of my favourite things to do. Occasionally I would bring to work food that I had baked or made myself. Who doesn't love a homemade muffin or scone?

REMEMBER YOUR MANNERS: Yes, the simplest words of thank you or please can make a difference to someone. Some people can be so rude and mean; not everybody remembers to take their manners with them when they leave the house!

It's important to observe your thoughts and actions, and the words you speak about the people around you. Send out positive energy to others and be open to receiving positive energy in return. Focusing on gossip, rumours, pain, fear or sadness will not serve anyone.

The energy you are sending out to others can create obstacles for them in their journey through life. You don't know what can affect them as you never what know that person is struggling with. Just be kind to all people and make sure you're sending out good vibes.

Again, I understand that not everybody has the same heart as you. Not everybody will be kind, but there are simple little things you can do to make things kinder and more positive and harmonious around you. If you have to lie, cheat or do bad things, then maybe shouldn't be doing that. Can you afford to limit the blessings and good luck that come into your life? Are you willing to cop the brunt of your own bad thoughts or actions after sending out bad energy?

Make sure you set personal boundaries around what you will and won't tolerate. Offering to help somebody, avoiding gossip and saying thank you are just some ways to create and build harmony amongst others.

Ask somebody: Are you okay? Sometimes this can go a long way, as you never know what they are going through. Your kindness, support and positivity could mean a lot to somebody; but also keep in mind that if they need professional help and assistance, it may be best to leave it to the professionals. And remember that it is up to them to make the decision to seek the help they need.

Do a good deed for somebody, compliment them, shout them a coffee (for example). Brighten their day. Remember, your thoughts, the words you speak and your actions all come back to you. You never know what tomorrow might bring. Take action, show appreciation, show someone you care. Cherish the ones you love by simply doing a good deed, giving them a call or sending them a text message to see how they are doing in life and warm their heart. Be kind always!

Chapter Four

Don't Worry, Be Happy!

This chapter is all about happiness.

Before you read any more, perhaps we should ask some important questions.

What is happiness?

Happiness is internal. It comes from within you and is found within you.

How do you become happy? There are many ways to become happy. This is just one:

- Start by having some anticipation within your day and within your life. Be excited about what your future might bring, and see the possibilities in everything.

- Start out small and do simple things to feel better. Get out of bed tomorrow and write a list of what you can do in your day. If one of these things was making the bed and then brushing your teeth and that's all you managed to accomplish, then don't worry - be grateful that you did that.

- Then the next day, write that list again and try and accomplish it. Be grateful, and be happy about it. Keep practising this, as it is one way to build, create, or find happiness. Have gratitude and anticipation for the future, because happiness is found within yourself.

Everybody's perception of happiness is different. A vegan Ben and Jerry's ice cream will make me happy, but it may not make you happy because of the price. I am not worried about the price; I am enjoying the vegan ice cream. Positivity is a choice. I could worry about the negative - the cost of the ice cream - or I can choose to enjoy the happiness a tub of ice cream brings me!

> *That leads to another question.*
> *Can money buy you happiness?*

That is a debatable question and the answer depends on many things, such as your financial budget and your circumstances. I am not going to focus whether money can or cannot make you happy. In this chapter, I would rather focus on how to be happy.

Some things that can make you happy:

- Your car
- Children
- Family
- Your job
- Relationships
- Your pets
- Your family
- Your friends.

Towards the end of 2010, when I was 25 years old, I was diagnosed with depression and prescribed antidepressant medication. I understand how difficult it is to try and be happy when you are mentally unwell. It's not easy to find happiness or make your yourself happy when you suffering with a mental health problem. But there is one thing that will help you recover and feel better and find some happiness: laughter. Laughter is the best medicine.

Eventually all those little moments of happiness will become bigger moments of happiness.

Here is a little mantra to keep you upbeat and positive throughout your day. The Positive Pledge is good way to kick start your day or to use when your day has gone bad.

POSITIVE PLEDGE

I shall not allow negative thoughts or feelings to drain me of my energy.

Instead I shall focus on all that is positive in my life, I shall think it and speak it.

By doing so I will send out vibes of positive energy into the world, and I shall be grateful for all the wonderful things it will attract into my life.

Some ways to find and establish happiness:

ASK YOUR SPIRIT GUIDES: *How can I be happy again? What do I need to do to be happy?*

Pay attention to the answers to your questions.

FOLLOW ANY SYNCHRONICITIES: Pay attention to any sign or message the universe and your Guides send out to you. What is it trying to tell you?

MEDITATE: Find the time to meditate, be still and go within yourself. Meditation can bring answers and provide information. Just observe.

PETS: Animals are a great way to make yourself feel happier and cheer yourself up. Animals don't ask of you much more than a pat or cuddle every now and then.

COUNT YOUR BLESSINGS! You can always find something to be grateful for.

HELP SOMEBODY: You can feel happier and better by reaching out to somebody, doing something good for them, and being kind.

GET OUTSIDE: Going for a walk can change your mood. A brisk walk gets your heart pumping. Get yourself grounded amongst nature.

WRITING: Write down your thoughts and feelings. It's a good way to release what is within you, and you don't have to share or tell anybody. Could your happiness be found within your writing? The answers you seek or want could start to be found when you write things down.

One of my favourite sayings is "respect yourself enough to walk away from anything or anyone that no longer serves you, grows you or makes you happy". Happiness is not out there in the world - it's within you. That is where it begins. Don't forget to be happy whenever it's possible.

Chapter Five
Affirmations

"Affirmations" is a New Age word for positive thinking and self-empowerment.

Affirmations are short positive statements that you say to your subconscious mind. Saying affirmations will reinforce a positive mindset, thinking and habits within yourself. It's a way of building faith and confidence. It's not going to change your life instantly, but you could start to notice some good things happening in your life when you say affirmations. It's a step-by-step process.

I first started using affirmations back in 2010 when I had depression. It was towards the end of the two-year period when I discovered affirmations. I started saying these positive statements first thing in the morning, or when something bad had happened or I'd had a bad thought. I basically replaced a bad thing with a positive.

Affirmations need to be said daily. I prefer to say them every morning. It's up to you how you say them. You can say affirmations in your head, or speak them out loud or quietly to yourself. There are so many ways to use affirmations to improve your life - weight loss, self-confidence, work, family, and so on.

Affirmations will help to motivate you to take action towards things you want in your life, and they will help you to keep focused on the goals that you have set for yourself. Affirmations will help change your negative thoughts into positive thoughts, and help you feel positive about yourself.

My favourite affirmation is this one from Louise Hay:

> *It's only a thought and a thought can be changed.*

This affirmation is great for any time you think negatively, and it reprograms your thinking.

What happens if you've tried to use affirmations but it's not working for you? Here are some possible reasons for this:

- You feel like you're lying to yourself, and don't believe in your affirmation.

- You are trying to break a habit and you just can't seem to do it.

- You're not saying your affirmation daily.

You can find affirmations online through searches on Google, Pinterest, or Facebook pages. If you are searching for more affirmations, your local bookstore will have books within the Self-help or Spiritual sections.

I have learnt from experience that Louise Hay has the best affirmations. Dr Wayne Dyer is another famous American author who has written some good affirmations and thought-provoking statements to help assist in changing your mindset.

Here is a sample list of affirmations that may be beneficial to you or somebody you know:

HEALING: I release the hurtful past and move into the future with joy and enthusiasm.

HEALING/SELF-CARE: I am learning to take care of myself.

EMPOWERMENT: No one can make me feel inferior.

FRIENDSHIP: I have some good friends who enjoy my company, and I enjoy theirs.

LOVE: My partner appreciates me.

MONEY: I am open to wealth in many ways.

HAPPINESS: I am living my best life!

SUCCESS: I live my life without fear. I am an unstoppable force.

GRATITUDE: I am grateful for all that I have.

HAPPINESS: I am feeling happy and optimistic about life.

MONEY: I bless the money I have; it's safe to save money and let my money work for me.

SOULMATE: My soulmate and I are being drawn together.

I truly hope that this chapter has inspired you to try saying some positive things to yourself to change your mindset, because your thoughts create your reality. Find some affirmations that you like and say them to yourself. Good luck on your first step to positive thinking.

Chapter Six

Intuition

You may be wondering why there's a chapter on intuition in this book. Well, it has been included because your intuition can be helpful to you in many ways. Listening to your intuition is important, regardless of whether you are having a good day, or are caught in traffic, stuck making a decision, or going through a rough time, and so on.

Since I was young I have been very intuitive, and have tuned into my inner feelings and environments around me. It wasn't until I studied a spiritual course that I realised I had spiritual abilities.

I consider myself to be a highly intuitive person. In my first book, I mention my intuition and intuitive feelings through all the chapters. For me, intuition is knowing without knowing. For example, somehow I just "know" I should have turned right instead of left when driving; or I just have the feeling that I should have turned on the porch light at home because I won't be coming home until late.

Intuition is a good thing because it can help in so many ways:

- It helps you to read people and understand the type of person somebody is

- It can be helpful in decision making

- It helps release Karma

- It is good for setting goals for yourself

- Where there is a potential danger, your intuition could put you on alert and warn you.

- It can help you to align yourself to your true path.

It's easy to fall into the habit of tuning out of your intuition. I am guilty of doing this myself!

If you do so, tap back into it, because it's a powerful personal trait to have. Some people listen to their intuition and use it more effectively than others, and then there are others that don't listen to their inner dialogue at all!

Here are two ways to tap into your intuition:

JOURNALLING: I know I mention this a lot, but it's a good way to notice things about yourself. You will look back through your journal in the future and reflect upon your thoughts and feelings.

TAKING YOURSELF AWAY FROM THE SOURCE OF STRESS FOR A WHILE: Tune back into yourself by clearing your mind, and focusing on your breathing. Is it going too fast?

Do what is best and right for you, by listening to your inner dialogue and not being swayed by other people's opinions and viewpoints. Listening to your intuition is trusting that gut feeling you may have, being mindful, paying attention to your dreams at night. What are they telling you? Pay attention to your emotions, as they can leave you with clues about what you can do about things in your life. Meditation can also assist in tapping into your inner knowing.

Sometimes getting the answer you need may not come from anywhere else, but from within yourself. Trust your intuition - it never lies. Never underestimate the power of your own intuition. Hopefully you will tune into your inner knowing after reading this. What is it telling you?

Chapter Seven

Just Be Yourself

Life is full of ups and downs, and life wasn't meant to be easy. We all have hopes, dreams, and goals around what we like and how we want our life to be. But things happen, things like major life changes or feeling stuck, lost or out of place. And sometimes we find we have a new outlook on life.

Self-confidence is required when it comes to:

- Finding your authentic self

- Having the self-confidence and courage to make some changes for yourself

- Developing the ability to trust your own judgement and abilities

- Knowing that you are worthy and valuable

- Making these changes, and

- Owning your mistakes, flaws and imperfections.

As we go through life we change. If you don't change you won't grow.

Here are some ways to discover yourself and learn more about who you are as a person:

TRUST YOURSELF: Have confidence and self-esteem. Know you are making the right choices or decisions, and if things go wrong you can learn from them. Be positive about situations that scare you, and know that you will get through.

FEEL COMFORTABLE: Feeling uncomfortable around certain situations or people is a good way to gauge your strengths and weaknesses. Your tolerances tell you about your likes and dislikes.

TRY JOURNALLING: Writing down your thoughts, emotions and feelings, your eating habits, exercise routine or sleeping habits and patterns, all help you to figure out the type of person you are.

LET GO: Sometimes we hold onto the familiar or stick to our comfort zones to feel safe. We need to let go of some things in order to welcome in new things.

ACCEPT YOURSELF: Accept your flaws and imperfections. Some things will change for you and some things will remain the same - this is something you may have to accept.

MEDITATE: Once again, meditate. Try finding the information and answers that meditation can bring. Calm your mind, body and soul by meditation.

FEEL HAPPIER: Just start feeling happier in general - anything from your thoughts, feelings, moods, etc.

HAVE A SENSE OF PURPOSE: Do something you like or enjoy; go to places you like, etc.

MAKE CHANGES: Learn what you like and dislike, then make changes according to those likes and dislikes.

BE GROUNDED: Go outside, get some fresh air, hug a tree, lean up against a tree, take a salt bath or meditate.

LISTEN TO YOUR EMOTIONS: It's going to feel odd and weird with the changes you make. Listen to your thoughts, feelings and emotions. What are they telling you? What's right or wrong? What feels good or bad?

MAKE A BUCKET LIST: Think about all the things you like to do, want to do or have never done before and would like to. Write these down in a bucket list and start to make them happen.

Here are some questions to ask yourself when learning about yourself:

- What do I like to do?

- What won't I do?

- What type of person am I? A morning person? A night owl? A people person?

- What are my personal boundaries?

- When was the last time I made some changes for myself?

I rediscovered who I was after losing everything. It took a couple months of feeling lost, but I found my authentic self. It was a sad, scary and daunting period, but I got through it, and you can get through it too!

I have a sense of humour, I am kind, caring and loyal to friends and family. These are just some of the things that I started to discover about myself. I wrote everything down on paper, trying to create, re-invent myself.

- What of personality traits do you have?

- What makes you unique and defines who you are?

- What are you going to change about yourself?

- Is there something you'd like to change?

- Are you happy just the way you are?

Authenticity is the courage to be yourself, so be brave and bravely be you. Have the courage to be yourself!

Chapter Eight

Bad Readings, Phonies and Dream Catchers

The best psychics or spiritual people can be found through word of mouth. Here in this chapter is an account of some of my experiences, my insights, and how not to get caught up in wasting your time and money on a reading, only to find out it was a bad reading or a fake psychic. Not everything is as it seems.

Bad Readings

I am going to be honest: I have done some bad readings in the past. I feel guilty about this, but when you're starting out you will make some mistakes along the way. Sometimes things just don't work, and they can go wrong for many different reasons. People aren't always truly open to a psychic reading; they might say they are, but the psychic can't connect properly with them. Sometimes the psychic reader isn't using all their senses and it is not a good reading, and unfair for the client.

A good reader, psychic or medium shouldn't instil fear into you. They also shouldn't tell you that you are cursed, or that you need a curse removed and you need to pay extra for it. If this happens to you, you should say no and walk away from the reading. You should be left feeling refreshed, inspired and uplifted by the reading and the reader. You should also be feeling positive, and positive about yourself.

One day I was at a market stall which I had set up for the day at a spiritual and wellbeing market in the north-west part of Melbourne. There was a man at the market, a young man in his early 20s who was just wandering with no sense of direction or plan on what to do. He was wandering up to stalls, then walking away quickly. It was odd as everybody else was wandering up to stalls and browsing and talking and looking at the stalls, but not this guy. He eventually made his way to my stall, and by this time my intuition just knew he was trouble and that something wasn't quite right about him.

When he walked up to my stall, I said hello and asked if I could help him. He explained that he had some "bad stuff attached to him". My clairsentience and empathy were telling me to feel sorry for him, but to say no and that I couldn't help him. The reason that I said no was because I knew that whatever bad entities he had attached to him, those bad things would have to go somewhere. I am not just writing this to be funny

- it is true! I don't want bad energy or entities to be attached to me or one of my clients, and then give a bad reading. I suggested there might be someone else who could help him, and that a market stall wasn't the right place to be removing attachments from somebody.

Phonies

Spirituality and the New Age have been trendy for a few years or so now, with the popularity of such things as yoga, meditation, tarot readings, holistic wellbeing, and so on. As a client, you need to know you can trust the information you receive from a spiritual person, and that what you tell them is safe. There are people who claim that they're "talented" or "gifted" in the work they do, but not everybody is gifted as a spiritual person. I am not gifted as a medium who can communicate with the dead who have crossed over. That's not my purpose or calling. So be careful who you are opening up to. They are a horrible person if they misguide you. I have caught up with a few fake psychics, and I was lucky enough to figure them out through my own spiritual abilities.

How often should you get a reading?

It all depends on you and your circumstances, and what has happened in your last reading. Was it accurate for you and your circumstances, and has anything happened since your last reading? Whether or not you act on your insights is at your own discretion.

Your connection with yourself and your reader affects your reading itself as well as the outcome of your reading. A good quality of connection, and being open to a reading and the insights, will give you a good quality reading.

Psychic Addiction

Are you visiting too many psychics or following too many spiritual people or threads on social media?

This can be overwhelming and confusing for you, with information overload. You may have doubts about your circumstances and go searching for what you want to know or hear. It can affect your self-esteem and self-confidence, and you may find yourself with anxiety about something in your life. One psychic will predict something, then another psychic predicts it won't happen, and yet another psychic may predict with certainty; in the meantime, you're following all three psychics and you are left feeling a little confused. Again, it's about using your own discretion. If you feel you aren't worthy or not enough, receiving a whole bunch of information or answers will affect your own judgement and clarity.

- What are your gut feelings telling you?

- What is your mind telling you?

- What is your heart telling you?

Some spiritual people will read their cards, messages and insights in a general and collective manner. But a collective reading will not resonate with everybody; it may resonate with some people or not at all. Some people may be disheartened by this, especially if they are stuck in a situation, or confused about their circumstances and have been searching or psychic-hopping until they find the message or answer they want. Another reason someone may do that is for the attention it brings from the psychic and their other followers, which is unfair.

Allow time and space for things to happen in your life. Allow time for things to manifest, and don't try and force things to happen.

Following spiritual people on social media is an energy exchange as well, and it's not good when the energy isn't right! There can be some trashy vibrational energy on social media, so make sure you're following genuine and reputable spiritual people and not phonies. When you are confident of the quality of the accounts that you follow and to which you give away your energy in your digital space, it can uplift your spirits and thoughts, educate you, and push you towards your achievements. On the flip side, it can be overwhelming or draining and confusing, and the vibrational energy may be too high for you.

As a spiritual person, I can find it annoying and frustrating when people follow someone and jump online begging for validation of their problem or circumstances. Sometimes they just won't stop asking, and they become upset and rude when the spiritual person doesn't respond. Again, it's an energy exchange. Make sure that where you become involved, it's positive and healthy. When spiritual people online are putting out their work, some people will appreciate it but some people will ruin it for others. What I am referring to are the comments on Facebook or Instagram, whether they are live threads or comments on posts.

Some signs of psychic addiction:

- Asking the same question more than once, and hoping for the answer you want

- Hopping from psychic to psychic for a reading, until you are happy with what you hear

- Having a reading again and again for the same problem

- Being unable to wait for a situation to resolve or fix itself, so you scroll through social media, call up psychic hotlines or purchase online card readings for an answer to the problem.

Listen to your own inner guidance, your thoughts, feelings and intuition; they will navigate your through your circumstances in life.

There's nothing wrong with seeing a psychic or following a spiritual person online. But my question is: how much is too much? When is it becoming unhealthy?

Dream Catchers

A dream catcher is a hanging circular object with feathers, string, shells and crystals hanging from it. Dream catchers are "sacred hoops", and they are supposed to protect you from bad and negative energies and nightmares when you are sleeping.

My little sister saw a dream catcher in a shop and fell in love with it. When you fall in love with something at a shop, there's a good chance you'll buy it! My sister bought this one and took it home and hung it up in her bedroom.

Some time had passed - maybe two weeks - and suddenly my sister was experiencing bad dreams, flickering of the lights in her bedroom, and ghostly encounters. My family couldn't work out what was going on. Yes, there was spiritual activity, but why so abruptly?

My sister's bedroom was upstairs in the house, along with three other bedrooms, but soon as you walked up the stairs you began to feel uneasy and experienced bad vibes. When I came to visit, I couldn't stay upstairs too long because when I walked up there the energy and bad vibes were so strong and powerful. Yet I couldn't pinpoint what it was at the time. I'd had many spiritual encounters before and I had seen couple of ghosts upstairs in my sister's room, but this time I questioned my own instincts and was in disbelief that one ghost could be so strong and powerful.

Then one day my uncle came to visit and he removed the dream catcher, and there was no more spiritual activity. It just suddenly stopped, vanished!

This is my family's experience with a dream catcher. Just be careful when you've one got - hopefully your experience isn't been as bad as this.

I have shared this information and these experiences in case it may be of benefit to you or to somebody you know. Make sure that you see and follow psychics who well known, popular or famous.

Chapter Nine

The Unemployment Blues

In my life I have spent some time being unemployed, and this is where my inspiration for this chapter has come from. Surely I am not the only one who is or has been unemployed and struggling. I understand this chapter isn't exactly as spiritual as the others, but the information I share might just help somebody else.

I hope these tips will help you if you are experiencing this:

KEEP BUSY: Create a routine of things to do for each day and the whole week. It may include:

- Following up on job opportunities or looking for a new job opportunity

- Taking yourself out for a walk, getting some exercise

- Maintaining your life and not getting stuck in mundane things like household chores.

Don't be still for too long, just keep being proactive.

SAVE MONEY: Saving money when you are unemployed can be hard, but your bills and expenses keep coming. Start saving $5.00 or $10.00; it's a start and it will all add up in the end. Save for your future and your future expenses the best you can. You don't want to be blindsided when you get an unexpected bill or expense to pay. Having something to contribute shows you are trying to better yourself, and some savings are better than no savings.

MEALS: Create a meal plan for the things you may like to eat for the next fortnight. From this meal plan you can budget how much money you'll spend, need, or save on groceries. From this step, allow for large portions of the meals from your meal plan, then cook the meals, ration them out and freeze them for another time. Meals that will freeze well are things like stir fries, mince dishes, casseroles and soups. I have done this for myself as a single person and it has benefited me many of times. On a few occasions I hadn't had to go grocery shopping again for that whole fortnight!

KNOW WHO YOU ARE! A job interview is a scary and nerve-racking experience, and the people who interview you can appear to be mean, harsh or difficult people. But they are just doing their job, which is to find the right person for the vacant position. Don't take anything to heart too much. Remember what your strengths and weaknesses are and what personality type you have, and learn what you are good and not so good at.

DO WHAT YOU LOVE: Doing something you enjoy will make you happy, and sometimes it could make all the difference. You'll be working all these hours and days in a job, so you want to enjoy it and make the most of it. Find something that eventually will take you to your dream job or career.

RECORD KEEPING: Keep a record of your job search efforts and history. When you are on the unemployment benefit, it's a government requirement to keep track of the jobs you apply for. Write down everything: the day you applied for the job, date, time, person you spoke to, and contact details such as a phone number and email address.

KARMA: Yes, karma has a role to play when it comes to being unemployed and looking for work! Don't let people around you bring you down or take advantage of you just because you're unemployed. How they treat you is their karma, but your goal is to get a job, so you need to have a level of professionalism about you. Being unemployed is a delay in your bigger picture. Try not to get angry or upset with people and situations, although it can be challenging at times. How can you be a better person from this downtime? What can you do now that your future self will thank you for?

A PLACE OF LACK: It's so easy and tempting to go into a head space where you think in terms of a "lack of". Once again, such a mentality will resonate and project outwards into the world around you, then onto other people, and they will notice. Think positive, be confident, and know that eventually you will have a job.

TAKE CARE OF YOURSELF: Look after yourself the best you possibly can.

- Make sure you get enough sleep at night and have enough energy for the next day.

- Eat healthy and don't skip meals - there's nothing worse than a grumbling tummy during a job interview!

- Have a rest day from your job hunting now and then, and spend some time with friends and family.

- Don't isolate yourself. Talk to friends and family about your situation and your job-hunting efforts. Don't keep it all inside. It can be a rough time being unemployed.

These are just some suggestions for you to use at your own discretion. It's up to you to choose whether or not to act upon the ideas. I am sharing them in the hope that it will benefit somebody in their quest to find a job, and that it will make a difference for them.

If you need advice, support or assistance, don't forget that there are organisations that can help unemployed people whilst they are jobless.

Chapter Ten
How to Deal with a Toxic Person

In this chapter of the book, I mention the dark period of my life, a 10-month period where I dealt with toxic people and a narcissist. This isn't a chapter I really wanted to put into this book. The word "narcissist" now just makes me cringe. I despise that word now. But when I stopped to think about it, I realised that surely I am not the only person to have a hard time dealing with somebody difficult, and I remembered that my purpose in writing this book is to help people.

I intuitively knew that I was going to be in trouble with this person, but I was helpless and powerless to stop myself from becoming involved. The only way I can describe how I became caught up in this mess is that it all started the moment this toxic person laid eyes upon me, and it was already too late for me!

I cannot tell you exactly what happened to me, because what the narcissist and her fellow helpers did were criminal activities and unlawful behaviour. But what I dealt with was extremely hurtful and heartbreaking. The narcissist created an elaborate hoax against me, saying vicious, deceptive and untruthful things and about me, and turning lots of people against me. That's what narcissists do. They start exaggerated lies based on suspicions in their delusional mind, and make false accusations. In my case, it resulted in damage to my reputation within my local community and I was hated.

There are two sides to every story, so don't be quick to judge a person without fully understanding the whole situation. It angered me that there were no consequences for the person's actions, and that they just kept on going, continuing their attacks against me. If you haven't done anything wrong then you shouldn't have anything to worry about. But the tactic was cruel and manipulative and left me with no evidence or proof to provide to a lawyer or the Police.

I prayed and prayed for many things. I said many affirmations to try to keep my thoughts positive and to have hope within this situation.

I am a spiritual person, and being also empathic, I felt sorry for the toxic person. I cared for my narcissist despite knowing that what was happening wasn't right. I was sucked into this situation and I became trapped. So began the narcissist-empath connection. I can't say it was a relationship because I never felt any love towards this person. Empaths are kind, compassionate, understanding and giving people. A narcissist is the total opposite; they thrive on taking, and they use their victim in any way possible, spiritually, mentally, physically and emotionally. Don't feel bad about yourself if you're in a situation like this and are feeling drained and depleted on these levels; this is what toxic people do.

Another challenging time was when the toxic person would return to my house, knocking on my door to speak to me, saying: "I've missed you", "I just want to talk", "I have changed and I have learnt from my mistakes". It's hard. You would hope they have changed and that you can believe their promises of a fresh start. But are you just going back to make the same mistakes twice? In this situation, you need to consider all the pain, agony, heartache and trouble this person has already put you through. Is it worth it to try all over again?

Stay strong. It pulls on your heart strings, and plays with your mind and emotions. But have no contact with that person. That's right - no contact! This toxic person failed on the first visit to my house, then sent two strangers to my house, who knocked on my front door for asking if I would like to speak to the toxic person. Again I was clear - no contact!

So many horrible and cruel things had happened to me, and I was innocent in all this.

Listed below are all the things I did that helped me to survive and conquer:

BLOCK: Block the toxic person, the bully, and anybody else that's involved in giving you a hard time. Block them on social media - Facebook, Twitter, Instagram. In all platforms where they have access to you, block them. Block their numbers on your mobile phone, to stop them from calling and texting you. This block applies in real life too. Seeing the person will be no good for your mental health and wellbeing. Don't speak to them - it will only come back to bother you afterwards. If you make eye contact, quickly avoid them and walk away.

DON'T REACT - RESPOND: Believe me, it's really hard sometimes, but as much as you want to react with anger, hurt, and out of pain, it will affect you. It will keep happening each time you react, and it's not healthy for you. It's what the bully or toxic person wants you to do. They want you to react. Please don't.

RAISE YOUR VIBRATIONS: Bullies or toxic people try to bring you down and affect you on so many levels – mental, physical, emotional and spiritual. Raise those vibrations the best you can, and rise above it. It's hard to feel good about yourself and your life, when people are hating on you and trying to bring you down. But raising your vibrations with positive thoughts will eventually give you a positive outlook. Watch funny YouTube videos, comedians or movies, for example. The bully will be wondering why you aren't crying or angry with them. Here is an affirmation that could help during your difficult time: *I will defend and protect myself no matter what.*

KEEP IN TOUCH: Keep in contact with family, relatives and friends. This is important when you are going through a tough time. At least somebody will know how you're thinking or feeling. Whatever you're going through and dealing with, you need to vent - don't keep it bottled up inside of you. I had a moment when a friend said to me, "You are not alone." This was a powerful phrase and it really helped me. It's true that you don't have to do this alone, so reach out to somebody!

FLIP THE CONVERSATION: This trick doesn't always work, but when it does it's good for you and you don't reveal anything about yourself. People will want to know how you are, but are they fake friends or flying monkeys? Flip the conversation, so it backfires onto them. Ask them questions about themselves and their lives. Remember that what you did at the time was what you thought was right and best for you at that time. Don't go back thinking, "What if? I should have done this or should have done that." You are only replaying the scenario over and over in your mind, and it's not healthy.

PRIVATE INVESTIGATORS: If you find that private investigators are following you, be aware that they normally travel in two separate vehicles. They will be costing a lot of money for whoever hired them. Take notes of their vehicle details, registration, and a description of the investigators. Don't be surprised if don't see them again; you may see a different investigator if they have figured out that you aware you're being spied upon. This happened to me. I have a sense of humour and I had fun with them and wasted their time by giving them no evidence and driving around roundabouts twice to make them lose track of me and stop following me. But I wouldn't really recommend it.

BE HONEST: Don't tell lies to make your situation better or to obtain a specific outcome. Tell it how it is, say the truth, say the facts and recount events as they happened. Lies catch up with you, and the truth comes out eventually. Karma knows everything! If you want come out the winner in the situation, be honest.

SAVE MONEY: When a situation gets really messy, that money you've been secretly stashing away is going to come in handy for your getaway to safety. You can use that stashed money for an Uber, a taxi or motel. It will come in handy and get you away from any harm or harmful situation. Have a trusted friend or relative on stand-by to help you when things get life threatening or it is dangerous to be at your home.

PRAY: Don't underestimate the power of prayer. Prayers don't go unnoticed or unheard. Eventually they have an effect. Sometimes the results of your prayers happen behind the scenes and you're unable to see them. There are many prayers to say, for many different circumstances.

WHITE LIGHT PROTECTION: White light protection is used by an Archangel within the spiritual realm to shield, protect and guard you from anything negative. The Archangel Michael can provide this protection. Just ask.

SET BOUNDARIES: Set boundaries for everybody in your life. You need to take care of yourself, heal, recover, and gain your strength back. So if sleeping in the morning is a luxury you like and you can do it, then make sure you can do it without being disturbed. Put in place personal boundaries such as trust, honesty, respect.

SAY AFFIRMATIONS: Do your best to keep your thoughts and your thinking positive. It will help you get through your tough time.

DO A CUTTING OF CORDS: A cord cutting removes any spiritual and energetic cord attachments between you and the other person. It will assist you in moving on and letting go of this person and removing them from your life. A cord cutting is something Archangel Michael will do for you when you call upon him in prayer. When needed, I have recited a cord cutting prayer twice a day: in the morning and at night, before bed.

DOCUMENT ANY EVIDENCE: Keep as much evidence as possible: video footage, photos, notes the bully or toxic person has written to you. Keep a record of incidents that have happened and document everything the best you can.

In another chapter of this book there is an Angel Prayer for Justice that may be useful for you in getting through your difficult time. I happened to discover it in the early days of my difficult time.

I can't stress this point enough: if you are dealing with a narcissist, toxic person or bully, whatever plans you make, whatever needs to be done, do it covertly so these crazy people don't ruin it for you. If you have confided in somebody who will help you through this time, that's great; but it could make the toxic person jealous and envious. It's something to be mindful of.

You don't want to be hurt time and time again, and you don't want to make the same mistake twice.

For me, the hardest part in dealing with all this was that my spiritual abilities meant that I knew who was involved and who was the mastermind behind all this chaos. It was hard because in order to take action, I needed some physical, tangible evidence to prove that these people were involved - not just my spiritual abilities. This was the frustrating part of my ordeal. I am psychic and I know things to be true, but then people will say: "Where's the proof?" It was so hard trying to get them to understand.

I wish you all the best if you happen to be dealing with a toxic person or bully. After all I have been through, I have survived. So whatever you are going through or dealing with, I really hope the information, tips and tools I've just shared are a part of your survival guide. I hope you heal, recover, let go and move on, as I did, to live your best life.

Chapter Eleven

A Little Less ...

In this chapter I want to talk about how much we expose ourselves to media like TV, radio, billboards, advertisements and social media, and their effects on us. The media will try to influence us or persuade us to change our views, opinions, thoughts and feelings about current events, political views and so on. It's okay to change your mind, but it's also important to stand your ground for the beliefs, values, and opinions that are important to you.

We can control how much we expose ourselves to media, but it's also important to keep in touch with what is happening around us. How do we find that balance? The answer is that it is a personal choice and decision.

Here are some helpful things to try, if you would like to make some changes in your life. You can reduce your media exposure by:

- Limiting how much news you watch on TV

- Using a timer to lock you out of apps after a certain time

- Scheduling time for social media

- Giving up your paid subscription TV - you're paying to watch TV and sometimes life gets busy and you don't have time to watch what your subscription is paying for

- Having quiet time in your car, with no noisy music playing and no noisy, repetitive advertisements blaring out at you.

Some of the benefits of exposing yourself to less media are that you will:

- Feel more accomplished, because you will have more time to do things

- Know who your real friends are when you have less online presence; you'll realise you have "internet friends" or "fake nice" friends, but the people who really care will call or text message you and socialise with you

- Have time to focus on other things in your life

- Start sleeping better

- Feel more motivated

- Feel less anxious.

How can you reduce the media in your life?

Watching TV in the morning can affect your mood and your morale for the rest of the day, depending on what's making news and what you've been watching. This is especially the case if current events are unfolding or something bad has occurred. It grabs your attention and sometimes it can derail you from preparing and organising yourself for the day. I enjoyed watching TV, and I spent lots of time on social media too. But I found that having the TV or radio on in the mornings was a distraction when I was trying to organising myself for the day. When the Coronavirus pandemic started, it was all over the media, and it was just too much. So I tuned out and found other things to do.

- How will you change your media exposure?

- Is too much media playing a big role in your life?

- If you are on social media, are you are happy on there too, and not just in real life? Remember that it's an energy exchange.

Chapter Twelve

Start A New Life!

Sometimes things get a little too much and every ending is a new beginning. Sometimes things just become overwhelming and you can't take it anymore. Sometimes you just outgrow people, places and things.

These are some things that you can do to make a change for yourself:

TAKE THINGS DAY BY DAY: There is no need to rush. Do not stress yourself out. Sit at home and plan in silence.

DO YOUR RESEARCH: Start planning. Figure out where you want to relocate to, then work out the costs for travel, removalists, toll roads, airfares, transporting your pets. How many possessions will you take?

FIND SOME NEW HOBBIES AND INTERESTS: Go to your local community centres and see what programs and activities they have to offer. Explore the local area.

CUT OFF NEGATIVE PEOPLE: People who are negative are either lonely, broke or bored. Sadly, the truth is that some people can't live life without a bit of drama or negativity. Remember that old saying: stay away from negative people as they have a problem for every solution.

LET GO! Not letting things go can be a burden and baggage you have to carry. If somebody wants to keeping fighting with you, bringing you down, let them but don't respond. Let it go. Leave it behind before you relocate to your new place.

HEAL FROM YOUR PAST: Forget about who did what and what was wrong, etc. Shift your focus to yourself. Whatever broke your heart, whatever hurt you, it hurts - but heal it. Patch up that wound and become positive and make the move to a new chapter or a new life!

WORK OUT WHAT'S GONE WRONG: Before you start a new journey, you need to know what's gone wrong for you and learn from it. It could be a job loss, bad relationships, and so on.

KNOW YOUR WORTH: Don't settle for less. You are worthy of love, you are worthy of success. Empower yourself, motivate yourself. It all starts and ends with you.

LOOK AFTER YOURSELF: Make sure you are eating healthy food and getting enough sleep, because moving can be a stressful and chaotic time. Look after yourself once you arrive at your new location, too.

TALK TO SOMEBODY: Share your ideas and plans with somebody trustworthy before you start making set decisions and moves, so everything goes smoothly. You want to get this right.

FORGIVE: I know this isn't exactly what some people want to do when they have been treated badly. However, it's sometimes good for yourself to forgive, even though you know they may not change their ways, and will continue those bad habits.

Sometimes you have that gut feeling or inner knowing and you just know that it's time to do something new and different. So trust the magic of new beginnings.

I hope these tips help you on your journey or any your changes you are making in your life!

Chapter Thirteen
Establish A Routine

Start your day off right.

- Do you roll out of bed in the morning?

- What time do you need to leave the house?

- Do you have a to-do list or schedule ready to go?

When I get out of bed in the morning, I have a ritual that I try to follow. It will be different for people who have children, of course. Everybody is different. It's about adapting your routine to you and your needs. But it's important to start your day right, as it sets the mood for the whole day. My routines are simple and I try not to rush in the morning unless I am running late for something.

When you establish a routine for yourself it helps you manage your time. This will bring you a number of benefits, For example, you may find yourself sleeping better, and you may become more efficient and self-disciplined, and be able to maintain a healthy balance in your life. You may run on time for work, and find yourself having to stress less in the morning rush at your household.

Most people these days check social media in the mornings, but it can be quite distracting. In checking everything, what you thought would be a 15-minute Facebook or Instagram check is now half an hour long and your morning schedule and routine is thrown out whack.

The gym is another trendy place to be in the mornings, to exercise and get fit. Or for some people it is a morning walk or run. It is something I used to enjoy doing, but it takes great motivation, self-esteem and self-discipline to be able to get up early to go and exercise in the rain or during cold weather.

Every morning as part of my routine, something that I do for myself is to say affirmations and prayers, before I even jump out of bed. Then, some time before 9 am, I will meditate for 15 or 30 minutes maximum.

I can't function through my day without some sort of handwritten to-do list or schedule. It keeps me on track with what I want to accomplish that day. It helps me to attend appointments without running late, or worse, forgetting about an appointment. Having my schedule also makes me mindful of where I am sending out my energy and putting in time. I am a worrywart. I have a diary and hardly use it; I have a calendar and I write all over it, but sometimes I forget to look at it. I save things in the calendar on my phone, then silence it because the phone keeps making noises. Sometimes a bit of paper and pen is the best way to keep a routine on track and accomplish things throughout your day.

I have also done this a couple of times too, which is fun - if you have a friend who doesn't join you throughout the day, it makes everything more enjoyable. Instead of being mundane and flying solo, you work together to accomplish errands that you both have to run, and complete tasks that you both need to accomplish within your day.

These are some just things I like to do throughout the week:

- Homemade tacos for Tuesday night's dinner

- Sleeping in on a Saturday - if my body clock lets me!

- Sunday mornings is pancakes for breakfast

- A Sunday road trip during the day, exploring the local area or countryside.

Set your phone so that it dims the brightness on your screen closer to bedtime, and mute notifications at certain times in the evening so you can unwind from your day. Depending on your phone, if you have repeated calls or messages from the same number or contact, they won't be muted. These simple little things can help with your evening routine and get a better night's sleep.

I say this bedtime prayer to myself before I go sleep at night (although sometimes I forget...). It is the same bedtime prayer that was in my first book. After a stressful day it can put your cares, worries and stresses at ease, then hopefully you will sleep well through the night. I am sharing it again in this chapter, because if do not have my first book yet, you may like to use the prayer before you go to bed tonight.

Angels bless and keep me
Angels guard me while I sleep
Bless my heart and my home
Bless my spirit as I roam
Guide and guard me through the night
Please wake me with the morning's light.

Thank you. Amen.

Sometimes it's okay not to have done something or have it all figured out. Every now and then your routine will blow off course. Some days you are going to forget to make the bed.

But hopefully this chapter has helped you to become more mindful of your daily routines and how much time you consume doing certain tasks.

Make time for what matters for you. Hopefully your morning will start off a little better if you establish a routine or make a change to your current routine. Good luck!

Chapter Fourteen

Prayers

PRAYER FOR HEALING

Dear God / Angels / Spirit Guides,
Please heal any fear-based thoughts I may have,
in any dimension and all directions of time.
Help me to flourish into who my
soul is calling me to be.
Let the Divine light shine.
I ask you to remove from me what's stopping me from
expressing my Divine magnificence
in body, mind and soul.

Help me to forgive anything that needs forgiving
and help me to release what needs to go.
Open me up to receive all the good
people and good things
that are waiting to come into my life.
Heal anything in me that needs to be healed,
both known and unknown, for all time.
Let me live a long, meaningful life.

Thank you for all you do for me,
even when it goes unnoticed.
Help me to experience the daily
miracles you create for me.
Please guide and protect me always.

Thank you. Amen

PRAYER FOR STRENGTH

Dear Angel of Strength,

Please give me the courage and strength that I need
to face all the challenges that are before me right now.
Wrap me in your mighty angelic wings
and protect me from harsh, negative energies.

Thank you. Amen

PRAYER TO THE ARCHANGEL MICHAEL, FOR INCREASED ENERGY

Archangel Michael, I ask you and your
helpers to come to me now.
Please cut away and release anything
that is draining me.
Help me to lift my energy to its natural
state of vitality now.

CORD CUTTING PRAYER

*This is the prayer I mentioned in the previous chapter,
for help in dealing with a toxic person*

Dear God / Angels and Spirit Guides,

I ask God, my Spirit Guides, to help me with this task.

I wish to free myself for all eternity
from (person's name),
so that both of us may go free from ties that bind
and all energy attachments from the past.
It's time to move past the experiences we've shared.

I am thankful for what I have learned
and lessons given,
but this attachment to (person's name)
is no longer needed
and is holding me back and affecting my "now".

With power I now ask for all cords to be cut,
for all energetic cords psychically connecting
the two of us be removed,
and dissolved to the original sender.
It's my intention that no more energy attachments
hook onto me from (person's name).
With forgiveness and peace, I release them to move
away from me
and move on, whilst I do the same.

I call upon Archangel Michael to surround
me and cut away any cords
and give me protection, and I ask that it
be completed and sealed now.
Please cleanse my aura of negativity
and negative emotions
and seal it with love.

Thank you. Amen

PRAYER FOR NEW BEGINNINGS

Dear God / Angels / Spirit Guides,

I am ready to make a fresh start and am willing to do what I need to do to accomplish my desires.
Thank you for helping me to stay focused on my goals and to embrace these new beginnings with enthusiasm, faith and joy.

Thank you. Amen

PRAYER FOR SUCCESS

Dear God / Angels / Spirit Guides,

I am ready to stand in a flow of abundance.
I ask that you send me clear signs as to
my best course of action to attract this prosperity.
Please help me to recognise, understand and follow these signs.

Thank you. Amen

Conclusion

To end my book, I would like to share some insights into myself, from some of the questions I am often asked.

- I am the only person in my family who is spiritually gifted. This can be a good thing and a bad thing. Members of my family do ask me about things on a spiritual level, and seek insight and opinions on what they should do in certain situations. I do feel grateful that I have been gifted with these spiritual abilities.

- Why am I writing books? I want to share my stories and knowledge with a wider audience than just a close circle of my family, friends and people I know. I want to be able to brighten somebody's day, to help in some way, and be able to help as many people as I possibly can.

- There are moments in which it is not so pleasant being psychic, but they are not horrible. There have been some challenging moments, and challenging times when I have not been able to read for my clients, for whatever reasons.

Being empathic and clairsentient makes it hard sometimes, too, because I can feel and sense what others are going through.

A shout out to all my followers and the supporters of my Facebook page, Cosmic Answers. Thank you for your continuous love and your support for me and my spiritual style and work.

A shout out to my friends and others in my inner circle who genuinely care about me - thank you, too!

Please check me out on Facebook by searching for **Cosmic Answers.**

So now you've just finished reading my second book. Where to next for me? I am cheekily and abruptly ending my book like this, keeping all my future plans a mystery!

Thank you for reading my book.

www.ingramcontent.com/pod-product-compliance
Ingram Content Group UK Ltd.
Pitfield, Milton Keynes, MK11 3LW, UK
UKHW042000230426
12048UKWH00009B/439